Napa Valley & Lake Tahoe Travel Guide

Attractions, Eating, Drinking, Shopping & Places To Stay

Oliver Bell

Table of Contents

Napa Valley

Vineyards dot California's Napa Valley (Wine Country) and tourists flock to the United States' premier wine-growing region, with its year round sunshine and quaint Napa Valley towns like Calistoga and Napa. This is a lovely area to visit the attractive and diverse wineries, while tasting fine wines to your heart's content.

Napa is the largest town and the surrounding areas are easy to reach by car including the nearby Sonoma Valley. Yountville offers fine restaurants, St. Helena has good shopping while Calistoga has an Old West quality.

Aside from the wine that makes this area so well known, it has many other attractions and activities. You can enjoy the nature of the area by biking, canoeing down the Russian River, or hiking.

Culture

Napa County has a population of 140,000, and is home to over 450 wineries. The Peak season is during the months of March to October.

Napa Valley is only 35 miles long and is easily navigated by car (but don't drink and drive.) Since the area is made up largely of farmland and vineyards, great food and wine can be found everywhere and there is no shortage of boutique shopping and nature to experience.

Napa Valley's wineries are commonly open between 10:00 a.m. and 4:30 p.m., and it is possible to visit many without an advance reservation. A fee is usually charged for tasting. Tours of wineries are educational and each winery is unique in its history and wine specialties.

Napa Valley is home to a number of fine historical buildings and is a good place to learn about California history (much of San Francisco was destroyed by an earthquake in 1906). Napa was founded in 1847, soon becoming a major site of the Gold Rush. The historic downtown has an historic mill, spa, restaurants, a jazz club, bakery and sweet shop, and an old-fashioned General Store.

Location & Orientation

The city of Napa lies 55 miles north of San Francisco; although some of the nearby towns have become more commercial, Napa has remained agricultural due to a land trust that protects the natural farmland of the area.

The Wine Country consists of a number of valleys and the Mayacamas Mountains. The Napa and Sonoma Valleys are on either side of the mountains; the other valleys nearby include the Dry Creek, Alexander, and Russian River valleys.

Gray Line bus tours run daily from San Francisco. Horizon Air has direct flights into the Charles M. Schulz Sonoma County Airport in Santa Rosa, which is a smaller airport, but closer than San Francisco or Oakland. Buses are available, but the service is very inconvenient. Of all the travel options in the area, travel by car is the easiest and smartest way to go. The roads are in good condition and cover the area, including highways and scenic back-routes. Since the area is relatively small, driving time will be short, even between towns. Travel time from one end of the valley to the other should be around 30 minutes, unless traffic is heavy, such as during rush hour or on weekends.

There are five major roads in the Napa and Sonoma Valleys: U.S. 101 takes travelers through Sonoma county, as do Routes 12 and 121; Route 29 (also the St. Helena Highway) runs north out of Napa, and the Silverado Trail runs parallel to Route 29 to Calistoga. The Silverado Trail, which is 25 miles long, is the scenic route, and has much less traffic. It is difficult to get lost in this area, and wineries are located all along the way. Pick up a map of the area at the Napa Valley Conference and Visitors Bureau.

 As for the location of wineries to visit, most of the major ones are located along Highway 29, while many of the smaller wineries are located along the Silverado Trail.

Climate & When to Visit

Any time of year is a good time to visit Napa Valley; the temperature is never too extreme, and there is always something to see - wineries are mostly indoors. If you are looking to experience sites like the Safari, kayaking on the Russian river, or other outdoor activities, you may want to plan a trip in the summertime.

Grape picking and crushing season is normally in September or October, and is dependent on the weather of the current year. There are all kinds of harvest festivals and fairs in the months of September through November. These include the Sonoma County Harvest Fair (complete with a grape stomp). If you are planning a trip during the busy season, it is smart to book any reservations at least a month ahead. When it comes to visiting wineries, earlier in the day is always better to stop by.

Every season in Napa has relatively nice weather, but each season is a little different and requires thinking ahead for packing and activity planning. Spring in Napa Valley begins in February and lasts through May; weather is variable. The temperature ranges from lows in the 40s and 50s to highs in the 60s and 70s (Fahrenheit). The rain isn't a problem when visiting mostly indoor wineries, but might be a hindrance if you plan on seeing sites that are outdoors. Rain is heaviest in February, although it is also the month when the vineyards are in bloom.

Summer is busy season in Napa, running from June through August; temperatures are in the high 70s and 80s. There are many summer festivals in Napa, including the Fair and plenty of concerts.

Fall in the area runs from September through October, and temperatures become cooler, going down into the 60s. It is a less busy time of year.

Winter in Napa Valley is rainy, with temperatures being in the 40s and 50s. Events this time of year include the Napa Valley Film Festival and holiday celebrations.

Sightseeing Highlights

Napa

Balloon Tour

www.calistogaballoons.com/
1458 Lincoln Ave. Railcar #15, Calistoga, CA 94515

Book a hot air balloon tour of Napa from a company with 30 years of experience.

The tours will take you through Napa Valley over vineyards and landscape, beginning early in the morning when the view is spectacular! You can see a lot of the landmarks you may not be able to visit, such as many wineries, Mt. St. Helena and Old Faithful Geyser. The company even offers free pick-up and return to and from hotels in Napa Valley. There are various packages available, including VIP private flights complete with champagne breakfast. The flight will be uncrowded and piloted by an experienced pilot dedicated to safety and comfort. The ride is one hour long, and you have the option of watching the balloon as it is inflated by the staff.

Tours begin between 6 and 7 a.m.; see the website for pricing and details.

Di Rosa

www.dirosaart.org/
5200 Sonoma Highway
Napa, CA 94559
707-226-5991

You may want to enjoy art on a visit to Wine Country. Visit Di Rosa, a gallery and nature preserve in Napa that has one of the biggest collections of Bay Area art in existence.

The art goes along with the theme of wine country; a lot of it is a part of nature and includes a historic winery. Tours are available, and prices for each tour range from $12-$15. They tend to last anywhere from 1-2 hours. Admission is free for children 12 and under, and there is a discount for seniors and students. Guests may visit the Gatehouse Gallery for free (donations suggested). See the website for hours and tour details.

Napa Firefighters Museum

www.napafirefightersmuseum.org/
1201 Main St
Napa, CA 94559
707-259-0609

If you have kids or are looking for more Napa history, the Firefighters Museum is a great place to stop for a visit. Over 150 years of history lie in the museum in the form of a collection of fire trucks and horse-drawn fire carts, engines, hydrants, toys, photos, newspaper clippings, uniforms and more.

The museum is open Wednesdays through Sundays from 11:00 a.m. until 4:00 p.m. Admission is free.

Wine Train

1275 McKinstry Street
Napa, CA 94559
www.winetrain.com

The Wine Train, located in Napa Valley, is a way to spend an afternoon, and is a great option for anyone, including families with kids. The train will give guests a three-hour historic tour of Napa to St. Helena, and goes through the towns of Yountville, Oakville, and Rutherford as well.

Tours are given with lunch or dinner, and food is provided, as well as wine. Winery tours are also an option.

The wine train is an excellent way to learn about the history of the area, as the train tracks have a long history and used to be the main form of transportation in the area. The train is an antique and has train cars dating back to the early 20th century. There are options of available tours on the Wine Train, and prices range from $134-$199 per person.

Safari West

$83 pp safari
9 & 10am
1, 2 & 4pm

www.safariwest.com
3115 Porter Creek Road, Santa Rosa, CA 95404
707-579-2551

With Safari West, tourists can go on an African Safari in the middle of wine country!

Visit this wildlife preserve that is also a privately owned home. Walk through an area of enclosures that house exotic animals, followed by an authentic automobile tour in the midst of the land where the animals roam free. The entire tour takes around 3-4 hours. There are over 400 animals in the 400-acre wildlife preserve. You will have the opportunity to see giraffes, antelope, ostrich, buffalo, wildebeests, cheetahs, lemurs, and more animals on the preserve.

Ticket prices for kids are around $30 and for adults are $70-$80 (depending on the season). Choose from a variety of educational tours. Lodging is also available with a set rate for tours and even an option for wine tasting!

Hess Collection Winery

www.hesscollection.com/
4411 Redwood Road
Napa, CA 94558
707-255-1144

The Hess Napa vineyards began in 1978, and the owner, Donald Hess, was was Swiss businessman whose art collection is contained in the museum. The vineyards now encompass 310 acres and the Hess Collection is known for its Mount Veeder Cabernet Sauvignon. The tasting room is open from 10:00 a.m. until 5:30 p.m. and visits are $10. There are free self-guided tours of art and production; see the website for coupon.

Domaine Carneros Winery

www.domainecarneros.com/
1240 Duhig Rd.
Napa, CA 94559

Inspired by the Chateau de la Marquetterie, a French mansion built in the 18th century, this winery will take guests to France with its architecture. It is a landmark of the area and is owned by Champagne Taittinger. The vineyard is certified organic, with wines almost entirely made from the fruit of the local estate.

Tastings are anywhere from $6.50-$85, and the "Art of Sparkling Wine" tours cost $30. Hours are from 10:00 a.m. until 6:00 p.m. Table service is a staple of the winery, and tastings may by paired with a selection of cheeses or caviar.

Artesa Vineyards & Winery

www.artesawinery.com/
1345 Henry Road
Napa, CA 94559
707-224-1668

Artesa Winery has a more unique look to others in the area; it is more modern. It is Spanish-owned and has many options of available wines, including Chardonnay, Pinot Noir, Cabernet Sauvignon, along with others that include Syrah and Albarino.

There is a $45 walk through the vineyard, as well as $10-$15 tastings and $20 tours. Hours are 10:00 a.m. until 5:00 p.m.

Bourassa Vineyards

www.bourassavineyards.com/

The winery, which is relatively new compared to some, is nevertheless one of the most well known in Napa. The owner began professional winemaking after forming a friendship with the godfather of wine in California, Robert Mondavi. The vineyard specializes in small portions of hand-made wines. The wines on which the company focuses include Cabernet Franc, Cabernet Sauvignon, Malbec, Merlot, and Petit Verdot.

Tastings are $20 and include current releases of wines, bottled water and crackers, and an explanation of winemaking, the role of oak and the cork. If you buy at least 2 bottles of wine, the tasting fee is waived. There is also the option of a $30 VIP tasting experience; they also offer more tastings, as well as various tours and other unique experiences.

Santa Rosa

Charles M. Schulz Museum

www.schulzmuseum.org
2301 Hardies Lane
Santa Rosa, California 95403
707-579-4452

A $10 tour of the Charles M. Schultz Museum will give visitors a glance into the world of the famed cartoonist whose comics have inspired millions. Schulz lived in Santa Rosa for 30 years, which is why the museum is located there. There are many ways for guests to learn about Schultz and his characters, including a re-creation of the studio where the artist drew his cartoons. The museum has a theater offering a variety of special films about Schultz and Peanuts; an education room where visitors can create their own cartoons, and an outdoor nature labyrinth of Snoopy's head. Located just across the street are an ice skating rink built by Schultz called Snoopy's Home Ice, as well as the Warm Puppy Cafe, where Schultz ate meals.

The museum is open from 11:00 a.m. - 5:00 p.m. on weekdays and 10:00 a.m. - 5:00 p.m. on weekends. There are a variety of self-guided and docent-guided tours available, and exhibitions are ever changing, aside from some permanent museum attractions.

Luther Burbank Home & Gardens

204 Santa Rosa Avenue
Santa Rosa, CA 95404
www.lutherburbank.org

Luther Burbank is a historical figure known for his work in botany; he lived at this home in Santa Rosa for over 50 years until 1906. Burbank is responsible for hybridisation of plants and developed over 800 new types in his day. The site is a great place to visit and walk through its beautiful gardens and greenhouse on a self-guided tour. Tours of the house are also available. The site is open from 8:00 a.m. until 5:00 p.m., and tour guides are available from April through November of each year. There are free audio tours that allow visitors to use personal cell phones and are free at specified times.

Arbor day is celebrated for Luther Burbank. He was friends with Henry Ford and Thomas Edison; the annual Santa Rosa Rose Parade is also celebrated each year to honour Burbank.

Calistoga

Old Faithful Geyser of CA

www.oldfaithfulgeyser.com/
Address: 1299 Tubbs Lane
Calistoga, CA 94515
707-942-6463

The Old Faithful Geyser erupts gallons of bubbling, boiling hot water and steam reaching at least 60 feet high every 30 minutes. It is a place to see when visiting the area because it is one of only three in the world that regularly releases water due to the conditions of the earth meeting all the specifications necessary. The geyser also predicts earthquakes. It has been seen on many TV stations and in a number of magazines and articles.

While visiting, there is a picnic area available as well a petting zoo with Jacob's Four-Horn Sheep, Llamas, and Tennessee Fainting Goats. There is also an exhibit hall and snack bar, along with a gift shop.

The geyser is open to visitors at 9:00 a.m., closing at 5:00 p.m. in the winter and 6:00 p.m. in the summer. Cost is $10 for adults, $7 for seniors, and $3 for children who are ages 6-12 (under 6 is free).

Petrified Forest

www.petrifiedforest.org/
4100 Petrified Forest Road
Calistoga Ca 94515
707.942.6667

The Petrified Forest will give visitors a sense a history and awe as they take a guided walking tour. The guides educate guests on the volcanic activity and how it affects the trees, geology, and plants of the park. Mt. St. Helena can be seen from the forest, as well as a mountain of ash that is 100 feet tall.

Hours are seasonal; the park always opens at 9:00 a.m., but in winter closes at 5:00 p.m. in spring and fall, at 6:00 p.m.; and in summer, at 7:00 p.m. See the website for a coupon that gives 10% off admission. Prices range from $5 for children - $10 for adults (free for kids less than 6 years old).

Sterling Vineyards

www.sterlingvineyards.com/
1111 Dunaweal Lane, Calistoga, CA 94515
707-942-3300

A visit to Sterling Vineyards differs from others, because Sterling has an aerial tram that goes up a mountain to reach the winery, the architecture of which is Greek because of the founder's heritage.

Atop the winery, visitors are able to experience panoramic views of the Valley. Tours of the winery are self-guided, and unlike other wineries, there are no large group tours offered. There are motion-activated TV screens that give explanations and serve as the "tour guide." There is even a fireplace in the tasting room.

The Sterling Winery is open weekdays from 10:30 a.m. until 4:30 p.m., and weekends from 10:00 a.m. until 5:00 p.m. Admission is $25 and includes the aerial tram ride, tour, tastings of five wines, and a souvenir wine glass. Under 21 fee is $10 (3 and under are free). You can also buy an upgrade for $30, the Silver VIP experience for $35, and the Gold VIP experience for $40. The website offers a $5 discount. It is also a Napa County Green Winery.

Castello di Amorosa

www.castellodiamorosa.com/
4045 Saint Helena Hwy
Calistoga, CA 94515
707-967-6272

Castello di Amorosa is more than just a winery; it is a 13th century Tuscan castle. Read about the history on the website - there is a book, with text and pictures, and is readable on the website. It is called *Castello di Amorosa: A History of the Project*.

The winery is open daily from 9:30 a.m. until 6:00 p.m. in the months of March through October, and until 5:00 p.m. November through February. It is only closed on Christmas day. Tours are over an hour and led by a guide. The Vineyard Tour is $33 for guests 21 and over, and $23 for ages 5-20. The Food and Wine Pairing Tour is $69 for adults, and not available to those under the age of 21. The Wine Aficionado Tour, which focuses on the high-end, specialty wines, is $49 for adults and not available to guests under 21.

Chateau Montelena

www.montelena.com/
1429 Tubbs Lane
Calistoga, CA
707-942-5105

This winery, which is a stone castle that is carved into a hillside, has grounds that reach all the way to the base of Mt. St. Helena. It is open from 9:30 a.m. until 4:00 p.m. each day. See the website for days closed. Regular tasting price is $20; the Library Wine Tastings are $40 and require reservations because they are limited to groups of six.

Chateau Montelena is unique because a Hollywood movie was made about it's famous Chardonnay in 2008; there is a special tour about the movie and history behind the Chardonnay, called "Beyond Paris and Hollywood: Untold Stories and Chateau Montelena Chardonnay." These tours are limited to groups of 12 and reservations are required. This tour costs $40 per person.

There is also a Vineyard Tour, which is $30 per person and limited to groups of seven; these are first-come, first-serve. There are a few other tours offered; see the website for details.

St. Helena

Culinary Institute of America at Greystone

www.ciachef.edu/california/
2555 Main Street
St. Helena, CA 94574

Along with wine, experience excellent food with a visit to the Culinary Institute of America at Greystone. There are many things for visitors to experience, such as touring the Greystone Winery, which is historical and has displays of cookware and cookbooks. There is also a Flavor Bar where you can participate in a tasting for $10-$15 of food. The Vintners Hall of Fame is also located here, which honors winemakers; weekend cooking demonstrations are available by reservation as well. There are 30-minute tours available of the building and all of its attractions.

On weekends at the school, guests can attend hour-long cooking demonstrations that are given by school instructors. These occur at 1:30 p.m. and include a glass of wine; they are $20 per person (free for those 12 and under). And, if you really want to learn more about cooking, you can take a class at the school. See the website for details.

The museum hours are 10:30 a.m. until 6:00 p.m., and the restaurant is open Sunday-Thursday 11:30 a.m. until 9:00 p.m., and Friday-Saturday 11:30 a.m. until 10:00 p.m. Tickets are $10 per person.

Beringer Vineyards

www.beringer.com/winery
2000 Main St.
St. Helena, CA, 94574
707-967-4412

Beringer Winery, whose founder, Jacob Beringer, came to Napa from Germany, focuses on education, offering more than just tastings: education on pairing wine with food, recipes, and more. They even have a culinary arts center on the property that is the mansion built by Beringer, and is on the National Register of Historic Places. The winery began in 1876, when tunnels were chiseled in the rock to be used to store the wines. The same tunnels are still used today. The winery is the oldest winery in Napa Valley that has been in continuous operation.

The Beringer Winery is open daily from 10:00 a.m. until 5:00 p.m., but is open until 6:00 pm. May 29-October 22. Tastings in the Old Winery Tasting room are $20; all tastings fees have a sales tax of 8.75%. There is a 30 minute tour that runs throughout each day that costs $25 (guests under the age of 21 are free). Reservations are recommended for the tour, and can be made online or by phone. There is also an hour-long tour, which occurs three times per day, and includes education on pairing wine with food. This tour is for guests 21 and over, and is $40.

Oakville

Robert Mondavi Winery

www.robertmondaviwinery.com/
7801 St. Helena Highway
Oakville, California 94562

The Robert Mondavi Winery, which began in 1966, is the producer of many wines that are known worldwide and have won numerous awards. They are best known for their Cabernet and Fume Blanc wines, and are Napa Green Certified, being the first to use organic farming methods in their vineyards.

The winery is also known for being one of the pioneers of wine tastings and programs, which are world-renowned. They are open every day from 10:00 a.m. until 5:00 p.m.; prices vary based on tours, ranging from $15-$55. Some of the tours include the Twilight evening walking tour, Wine and Music tour, Exclusive Cellar, Wine Tasting Basics, Discovery Tour, and Signature Tour and Tasting. Note that all but a couple of the tours are not intended for children. If you are looking for more options, they have additional Wine & Food Programs and Curated Experiences, which range higher in price for the most part.

PlumpJack Winery

www.plumpjackwinery.com/
620 Oakville Cross Road
Oakville, CA 94562
707-945-1220

Inspired by a character created by Shakespeare, this winery prides itself on being open and inviting to guests, encouraging people to enjoy wine and each other. and Open from 10:00 a.m. until 4:00 p.m. daily; tasting fee is $15. Although PlumpJack began in 1995, the estate has been around since the 1800s.

Rutherford

Inglenook

www.inglenook.com/
1991 St. Helena Hwy
Rutherford, CA 94573
707-968-1100

Inglenook was owned in 1975 by Francis Coppola, who had the vision to reconstruct the winery and restore its original vineyards. This project was completed and Inglenook is one of the most popular wineries in the area. Before Coppola, the winery had a unique history, beginning in 1879 when the designer, Gustave Niebaum, built a system that defied the science of its day.

The guided tour and tasting is $50 per person, and includes tastings of four wines with food pairings. This experience is offered three times per day and lasts 90 minutes. There are also many other tours and tastings, which range in price from $45-$95 per person. The Bistro is open daily from 10:00 a.m. until 5:00 p.m., and the Chateau is open daily from 11:00 a.m. until 5:00 p.m.

Grgich Hills Estate

www.grgich.com/
1829 Saint Helena Highway
Rutherford, CA 94573
800-532-3057

Grgich Hills is known for its famous wine, which has been used by Presidents at State Dinners; its owner, Mike Grgich, was inducted in 2008 into the Vinter Hall of Fame. This is a winery that has intentionally remained small throughout the years, focusing on the quality of the wine instead of growth and expansion. Because of this, the winery is known for being personable.

Hours are 9:30 a.m. until 4:30 p.m. daily. Weekdays and mornings are the best time to visit. There are a large variety of tastings available, with prices ranging from $20-$125 per person. Barrel tastings are included with any experience on most Friday afternoons from 2:00-4:00 p.m.

Peju Winery

peju.com
8466 Saint Helena Hwy, Napa, CA
707-963-3600
Cost: $15

This winery, is has a great location on Highway 29, has a house that dates back to the 1900s and historic vineyards.

It is a family business. Peju is a certified Napa Green Winery. The Gardens are an attraction in themselves, as they change daily.

The tasting room is open from 10:00 a.m. until 6:00 p.m. daily, with prices ranging from $20-$75 per person.

Recommendations for the Budget Traveler

Places to Stay

Marriott Napa Valley Hotel & Spa

http://www.napavalleymarriott.com/
3425 Solano Avenue
Napa, CA

This four-star, full-service hotel is in a convenient location - right off of highway 29 - and offers easy access to three airports. It houses a spa, 24-hour gym, laundry room, outdoor pool, wine and cheese tasting each day, beauty shop, restaurant and bar, and more.

Prices are from $199 per night, and the hotel is 100% non-smoking.

Napa River Inn

www.napariverinn.com/
500 Main Street
Napa CA 94559
707-251-8500

This hotel provides personalized breakfast delivery from a bakery. It also has a spa, restaurants, live music, and is located at the historic Napa Mill. There are evening wine tastings, free internet, a market and wine shop, a bakery, laundry, and more. Pets are allowed but smoking is not. The hotel consists of three buildings, one being the historic mill; the architecture is 1800s-style and the location boasts great views.

Prices from $229 per night.

Beazley House

http://beazleyhouse.com/
1910 1st Street, Napa, CA 94559
800-559-1649

This bed and breakfast is located on First Street and was the first bed and breakfast in town as well. It is an old Victorian mansion in a neighborhood that is conveniently located close to the West End, which includes the riverfront and other attractions. Amenities include free Internet, homemade breakfast, gardens, and more. Pets are allowed. Another plus is that the original owners still run the Inn, and are actively involved in the community.

Prices are $156 and up; it is best to book in advance for lower prices.

Best Western Premier Ivy Hotel Napa

www.ivyhotelnapa.com/
4195 Solano Avenue
Napa, CA 94558
707-253-9300

This four-star hotel has free wi-fi, a pool, fitness center, restaurant, hot tub, and continental breakfast. Prices begin at $127 per night. The hotel has high ratings. It is located in the wine region near hot springs.

Napa Inn

www.napainn.com/

This bed and breakfast inn boasts free wi-fi, breakfast, evening wine and refreshment, and in-room fireplaces. The inn is made up of two historic homes and also has a spa. The staff is personable and knowledgeable about the area.

Prices begin at $149 per night.

Embassy Suites Napa Valley

www.embassysuitesnapahotel.com/
1075 California Blvd.
Napa, CA 94559
707-253-9540

This hotel, located one mile from downtown Napa, has a resort design, inspired by the Mediterranean. They have free cooked-to-order breakfast, as well as free snacks in the evening. The hotel has a restaurant called Grille 29, outdoor and indoor pools, free access to a health club, and grounds that are landscaped. Prices range from $134-$300+. Pet suites are available.

Places to Eat

Bounty Hunter Wine Bar & Smokin' BBQ

www.bountyhunterwinebar.com/
975 1st St., Napa, CA 94559
707-226-3976

With free Wi-Fi, Happy Hour, and a Wine Bar, this restaurant is a good choice for lunch or dinner. Entrees are $15-$25 each. It also has extended hours: opens at 11:00 a.m. each day, and closes at 10:00 p.m. Sunday-Thursday, and 12:00 a.m. Friday and Saturday.

Celadon

www.celadonnapa.com/
500 Main St., Suite G
Napa, CA 94559
707-254-9690

Celadon serves different foods ranging from
Mediterranean to Asian to American, with outdoor dining
available. Prices are $15-$25 for an entree. Housed
downtown in the historic Mill, it is in a convenient
location. The restaurant is open for lunch and dinner;
hours are Monday-Friday, opening at 11:30 a.m. Dinner
begins at 5:00 p.m.

Bistro Sabor

www.bistrosabor.com
1126 1st St. Napa, CA 94559
707-252-0555

This Latin American restaurant is great for anyone,
including families. It is open for lunch and dinner from
11:30 a.m. until 9:00 p.m. on weekdays; Friday-Saturday it
is open until 10:00 pm. They also serve beer and wine
from local wineries. They even have Saturday Salsa
Nights, ever Saturday night from 10:00 p.m. until 1:00
a.m. for no cover charge (limited time). The restaurant is
closed on Sundays and Mondays. Prices range around
$10.

Zuzu

zuzunapa.com/
829 Main St.
Napa, CA 94559
707-224-8555

This Tapas Bar opens at 11:30 a.m. Monday-Friday, and 4:00 p.m. Saturday-Sunday. The restaurant puts a Californian spin on tapas as well as including menu items that are Mediterranean, Spanish and Portuguese. The atmosphere is one of the highlights of the restaurant. Prices range from $7-$15.

Alexis Bakery

www.alexisbakingcompany.com/
1517 3rd St.
Napa, CA 94559
707-258-1827

This bakery and cafe is a favorite of locals and is an all-inclusive place, with breakfast and lunch as well as cakes and pastries. The cinnamon bread is popular. Breakfast special prices are in the $14 range, and are things like "pumpkin pancakes with poached pears and pure maple syrup." Other breakfast options range from $7-$11.95. Hours are from 7:00 a.m.-3:00 p.m. Monday-Friday, Saturday 7:30 a.m.-3:00 p.m., and Sunday 8:00 a.m.-2:00 p.m. (no lunch on Sunday).

Centre Cafe

www.centrecafenapa.com
388 Devlin Rd
Napa, CA 94558
707-603-3260

Centre Cafe is a great place to eat food with locally made ingredients (in fact, as local as its next-door neighbor); breakfast is served from 8:00-11:00 a.m., followed by lunch until 3:00 p.m. Next is happy hour until 6:00 pm. It is open Monday through Friday. And, if you are going on a picnic, you can even purchase an express lunch of pre-made sandwiches and salads.

The cafe has baked goods, espresso drinks and French roast coffee for sale. They have a wide selection of foods, ranging from American to Mediterranean to Italian. Prices range from $7-$11.

High Tech Burrito

www.hightechburrito.com/
641 Trancas Street, Napa, CA 94558
707-224-8882

For Tex-Mex, visit High Tech Burrito; it is a southwestern-type place with a grill where you can choose what goes in your meal.

They have the usual burrito, taco, quesadilla fare, as well as original creations like the Burrito Dog: "All beef miller hot dog, melted cheese, pinto beans in a grilled flour tortilla." Another one is the Asian Pan Seared Shrimp: "Romaine lettuce, red cabbage, carrots, cilantro, tomatoes, green & white onions, cotija cheese, drizzled with sesame ginger dressing." They have Curry Shrimp, Braised Tofu Veggie Burrito, Ya-Hoo BBQ, Hawaiian Teriyaki, and more. Price range is $5-$10.

Places to Shop

Napa Premium Outlets

http://www.premiumoutlets.com/outlets/outlet.asp?id=25
629 Factory Stores Drive
Napa, CA 94558
707-226-9876

There are 50 outlet stores where you can shop till you drop at the Napa Premium Outlets, including Banana Republic, Tommy Hilfiger, Guess, Barneys New York, BCBG Max Azria, Calvin Klein, Coach, J. Crew, and many more. The outlets open every day at 9:00 a.m. and close on Monday through Thursday at 8:00 p.m., Friday through Saturday at 9:00 p.m., and Sunday at 7:00 p.m.

Oxbow Public Market

www.oxbowpublicmarket.com/
610 1st St.
Napa, CA 94559
707-226-6529

Also offering meals and wine while you relax and watch
the river, there are also produce stands and various local
merchants, such as bakeries, the Oxbow Cheese
Merchant, Ritual Coffee Roasters, Three Twins Ice Cream,
the Kanaloa Seafood Market, and more. There are various
restaurants and retail shops, as well as Napa Valley
Adventure Tours.

Bounty Hunter Rare Wine & Provisions

www.bountyhunterwine.com/
975 1st St.
Napa, CA 94559
707-255-0622

Complete with a wine bar, Bounty Hunter is the place to
go to find affordable rare wines and wine that is
becoming trendy ahead of time. Visit the website for a
coupon (limited time). This is owned by the same owners
as the Wine Bar & Smokin' BBQ restaurant; they are
"Wine Country Insiders".

Anette's Chocolate Factory

www.anettes.com/
1321 1st St.
Napa, CA 94559
707-252-4228

Anette's Chocolate Factory has a Napa history of 25 years
and offers specialty chocolates, gift baskets, come shop for
the perfect chocolate to pair with wine bought during
your visit to Napa. It is owned by a brother and sister
team who produce their own unique chocolates as well as
perfecting recipes that have been passed down for more
than 70 years.

Lake Tahoe

Lake Tahoe's crystal clear waters have long been a recreational retreat for the people of California and Nevada. During the peak winter season, Lake Tahoe offers some of the most sought after skiing and snowsports in the United States. During the warmer seasons, outdoors lovers visit for recreational activities including parasailing, kayaking, hiking, camping and fishing. At nighttime the action moves indoors to Lake Tahoe's many fine bars, restaurants, and casinos.

Lake Tahoe is a 22 by 21 mile fresh water lake, located on the border of of California and Nevada. It is a one hour drive from Reno, NV and can usually be easily reached by car, even in wintertime. It is about four hours drive from San Francisco, 3 hours from Oakland, and two hours from Sacramento.

The beautiful scenery around Lake Tahoe has long been the setting for wedding photographs and romantic getaways. The area's hiking trails are suitable for all levels of expertise and they lead to Lake Tahoe's hidden wonders, like Eagle Falls and other lesser-known lakes.

Lake Tahoe has a number of arts festivals and the region is blessed with excellent seasonal weather, making it an ideal year-round vacation destination. Lake Tahoe's North and South shores contain the main tourist attractions. During peak seasons, tourists triple the population of the area.

With one foot in Nevada, Lake Tahoe is situated in the most famous gambling state in America. The South Shore, in particular, is filled with large casinos. Back in the sixties and seventies, the casinos were favorite playgrounds for Frank Sinatra and the Rat Pack, the Kennedy's and movie stars flying in from Hollywood. The same happens today, so keep your camera at the ready.

The North Shore appeals to winter sports enthusiasts looking for downhill and cross-country snow activities. Squaw Valley is one of the most popular resorts and it hosted the Winter Olympics in 1960. North Shore skiing includes the resorts of Mt. Rose and Ski Incline and the resorts here are a little more isolated than the ski resorts on the South Shore.

Many movies have been filmed near to Lake Tahoe including Oscar-winner, *The Godfather*. It is also the location of the *Lake Tahoe Shakespeare Festival* held every summer, an event that attracts 20,000 visitors. Other local festivals include the *Lake Tahoe Chautauqua, Great Gatsby Festival,* and the *Festival of Fine Arts.*

Location & Orientation

Lake Tahoe is often referred to as the North Shore and the South Shore, with each shore located in both California and Nevada. Some tourists prefer the south shore given its accessibility to the population centers of California as well as its gentler slopes for the casual skier.

It's straightforward to reach Lake Tahoe by car from the gateway airports of San Francisco, San Jose, Reno or Sacramento.

Getting around Lake Tahoe is easy by car (except during the infrequent snowstorms) or you can take the Tahoe Area Regional Transit (TART) that runs along the shore and which operates regularly throughout the year. TART costs around $1.75 for a one-way trip. There are also water taxis which run between the north and south shores.

Climate & When to Visit

Lake Tahoe is enjoyable to visit year-round and is particularly popular during the summer and winter seasons. Summer in Lake Tahoe has an average temperature of 75 F, making it perfect for lazing on a remote beach or trekking up one of the mountain trails. Visiting in June to August is ideal if you want to catch a summer festivals.

In wintertime temperatures can hit freezing and snowfall is common (November to February). The average annual snowfall at the lake is 125 inches and at the alpine level and on the ski slopes ranges from 300 to 500 inches. This is prime ski-season and a fantastic time to visit.

Sightseeing Highlights

Squaw Valley

1960 Squaw Valley Road,
Olympic Valley, CA 96146

One of the more famous resorts on the north side of Lake
Tahoe is the internationally-known winter sports mecca
of Squaw Valley. Here you will find great ski resorts,
hotels and lodge accommodations, shopping and
restaurants.

You can visit the Olympic Museum at High Camp which displays memorabilia from the 1960 Winter Olympics which were held here. The Village at Squaw Valley is a pleasant center to the resort and has a commercial zone and much après-ski action. The Squaw Valley Adventure Center offers a variety of outdoor activities such as miniature golf, rope challenges, rock/wall climbing, and trampolining.

Incline Village

Located on the north shore of Lake Tahoe over the Nevada border is Incline Village, one of the best wintersports resorts. In addition to the skiing and snowboarding activities Incline Village is home to attractions like the Mark Twain Cultural Center (located on Mays Boulevard). The Mark Twain Cultural Center is both a bookstore and a theater. The Art Attack Gallery on Tahoe Boulevard houses work by local artists. At the heart of Incline Village is the Recreation Center with leisure facilities including beaches, sports halls, exercise rooms, a gymnasium, and a cardiovascular room.

Thunderbird Lodge (Museum/National Historic Site)

5000 Nevada 28 Incline Village
Crystal Bay, NV 89451
Tel: (775) 832-8750
http://thunderbirdtahoe.org/lodge

This museum was formerly the home of George Whittell, Jr. who once owned 40,000 acres of land in Lake Tahoe. The lodge offers guided tours of the grounds and tunnels. The site plays host to weddings, wine-tasting dinners at the castle, cooking classes, barbeques, and holds social events. Thunderbird Lodge accepts donations.

Diamond Peak

1210 Ski Way
Incline Village, NV 89451
Tel: (877) 468-4397
http://www.diamondpeak.com/

Diamond Peak, situated 35 miles from Reno Airport, is a beautiful mountain resort and is a great place for children or adults to learn how to ski or snowboard. Overlooking the north shore with a great view of Lake Tahoe, the resort operates from December to April at an elevation of over six thousand feet.

Diamond Peak has slopes that offer some of the largest vertical drops in the region with the longest downhill run being over two miles long. There are six ski lifts and thirty ski runs. Beginner Slopes: 20%, Intermediate Slopes: 45%, Advanced Slopes: 35%

Sand Harbor Beach

2005 Nevada 28
South of Incline Village, NV 89451
Tel: (775) 831-0494

For a modest fee you can enjoy the lake from one of the best beaches in Lake Tahoe. Parking can be a problem in high season and it is advisable to take the bus from Incline Village. Sand Harbor is a local beauty spot that offers a choice of water activities and has a number of small coves and rocky areas.

Glenbrook Cave Rock

U.S. 50, 4 miles north of Zephyr Cove,
Zephyr Cove, NV 89449
Tel: (775) 831-0494

Cave Rock in the Nevada State Park is a great place to relax, have a picnic and take a boat ride. There are barbecue/picnic areas near the beach and you can swim in the lake, fish as well as scuba dive. Making reservations for picnic areas is advisable, especially during peak season, but if want to make a quick stop you can purchase a pass at the park entrance; the price is $7-$12.

Lights on Tahoe South (Fireworks Display)

South Lake Tahoe, CA 96150
Tel: (530) 541-5255 or (800) 288-2463

The "Lights on Tahoe South" Fireworks display is one of best pyrotechnics displays held during the Fourth of July Independence Day celebrations and is visible from various locations around Lake Tahoe.

Emerald Bay State Park

El Dorado, California
Tel: (530) 541-3030

Emerald Bay State Park is home to Fennette Island, the only island on Lake Tahoe. The area is noted for its beauty in all four seasons. Here you can see local bears (which are protected and should not be approached). Emerald Bay offers camping, hiking, boating and other activities and has one of the best harbors on the lake. The temperature during the summer is around 70 degrees (F) during the day and can get as low as 40 degrees at night. During winter the temperature hovers between 20-40 degrees (F). The lake activities close during the winter. Emerald Bay State Park is directly south of DL Bliss State Park and you can take Hwy 89 / Emerald Bay Road to reach the location from South Lake Tahoe.

Vikingsholm

9881 Hwy 89
Tahoma, CA 96142
Tel: (530) 541-6498

Vikingsholm, formerly the summer home of Lara Knight, is a great example of 19th century American construction with a Scandinavian design. The entire structure was built using local resources. The 38 room mansion is a part of the Emerald Bay State Park and is accessible through the trail near the Harvey West parking lot on Hwy 89. Shuttle services are available from either the north shore or the south shore. Look for the clock referred to as "Selma" in the mansion. Tours are available at $8 per person, $5 for children.

Eagle Falls (Waterfall)

Hwy 89
South Lake Tahoe,
CA 96150
Tel: (530) 525-7277

While visiting Emerald Bay State Park, look out for Eagle Falls, a waterfall with beautiful cascading waters. Eagle Falls is a great place for photography enthusiasts and there is a pleasant ¼-mile hiking trail to Eagle Falls which begins at Emerald Bay.

Fannette Island

Lake Tahoe's only island houses an old teahouse that was built by Lara Knight of Vikingsholm fame. Fannette Island is also a popular place for wedding ceremonies. It is accessible by boat and is only a quarter mile from the shore.

Homewood Mountain Resort

5145 West Lake Boulevard,
Homewood, CA 96141
Tel: (530) 525-2922
http://www.skihomewood.com

Homewood is located close to Lake Tahoe and has great lake views from the ski lifts and downhill runs. Skiing courses are available for children and adults. Featuring eight chair lifts and sixty-four downhill runs, Homewood has more than 1000 acres of terrain. The resort mostly attracts intermediate skiers and snowboarders. One-third of the runs are advanced with only 15% of runs for beginners. Homewood is accessible via the Tahoe Area Regional Transit (TART) or if you are arriving by car you can take Hwy 89 to reach the resort.

Homewood Maritime Museum

5205 West Lake Boulevard,
Homewood, CA 96141
Tel: (530) 525-9253

Homewood Maritime Museum displays boats and other
watercrafts as well as various maritime artifacts. The
museum is run by a non-profit organization whose aim is
to build awareness of the maritime history of Lake Tahoe.
Tours are available year-round and the museum is often
visited by children on educational field trips. Local
experts will answer your questions about Lake Tahoe's
maritime history.

Heavenly Village

Heavenly Village Way
South Lake Tahoe, CA

Heavenly Village, located on South Lake Tahoe, is easily
accessible to many visitors driving in from California and
is filled with activity and entertainment. This is one of the
most popular resorts in Lake Tahoe and has great
restaurants, bars, shopping areas, skating rink, mini-golf
course, and an 8-plex cinema. It is a fantastic place to
spend your vacation. You can get there by following Hwy
50 to South Lake Tahoe.

Heavenly Village is filled with holiday decorations, festivities, (and Santa Claus) during the December holiday season. It's a great time to visit and ski conditions are typically good then. The skating rink is the perfect place if weather conditions deteriorate in wintertime. The entrance fee covers an all-day access pass and costs $15-$20 (depending on whether you need equipment rental). Fireplaces are lit near to the rink which add charm, particularly when the holiday lights are lit. The skating rink is only available during winter.

Heavenly Village is regarded as "the place" for shopping and dining in South Lake Tahoe.

Camp Richardson

1900 Jameson Beach Road,
South Lake Tahoe, CA 96150
Tel: (530) 541-1801
http://www.camprichardson.com/

Camp Richardson offers outdoor activities for the entire family. The bicycle course is popular and there is a lovely marina (open during the summer season). Choose from a variety of water-activities such as jet skiing, kayaking, paddle boating, boat rides, and more. It is possible for you to dock at the marina if you arrive by boat. There are also areas around Camp Richardson that permit camping. Camp Richardson is riddled with history as it once employed the local Washoe inhabitants of Lake Tahoe during its earlier years.

Nevada Beach State Park

Elks Point Road,
Zephyr Cove, NV
Tel: (775) 588-5562

The Nevada Beach State Park has the widest beach in all of Lake Tahoe (one mile). It is a lovely place to relax and to soak up some of the sun in the spring, summer or fall. Here you are only moments away from the restaurants, bars and casinos. Come here to spend the day before moving on to the nightlife. Simply relax or enjoy the adrenaline-fueled thrill of waterskiing.

There are dozens of campsites suitable for both RVs and tents, many with a view of the lake. Campfire pits and firewood is available to campers. Bears are known to frequent the area which is why the use of proper food containers is necessary.

Located near South Lake Tahoe, you take highway 50 heading east then turn left at Elks Point.

Recommendations for the Budget Traveler

Places to Stay

Rockwood Lodge

5295 West Lake Boulevard, Homewood, CA 96141
Tel: (530) 525-5273
http://www.rockwoodlodge.com

Centrally located in Homewood, Rockwood Lodge is just a stones throw from Homewood Mountain resort and the marina.

The lodge offers queen-sized beds, shower and tub with lake view, gear rental, and assistance with the booking of activities. It is close to establishments that offer golfing, rafting, fishing, hiking, water activities, ATV rentals and more. Restaurants are also close by. The room rates range from $125 - $225 per night.

Americas Best Value Inn

455 North Lake Boulevard,
Tahoe City, CA 96145
Tel: (888) 315-2378
http://www.americasbestvalueinn.com/

Americas Best Value Inn offers rooms with cable TV, wireless internet access, air-conditioning, complimentary continental breakfast, free parking, an arcade room, smoke-free rooms, an outdoor pool, and is within walking distance of the lake. The Inn has good views of the lake and is close to restaurants and other nightlife. It has 46 rooms and is located close to Tahoe City golf course and Tahoe City State Park. Access to the inn is easy as it is right on North Lake Boulevard. Nightly rates start at $26.

Inn by the Lake

3300 Lake Tahoe Boulevard. South Lake Tahoe, CA 96150
Tel: (800) 877-1466
www.innbythelake.com/

The Inn by the Lake is a great place to stay given its
proximity to the beach and nightlife and offers good
rooms at a fair price. In addition to the usual features they
offer an exercise room, a beach café, and complimentary
continental breakfast. The place is located just off
highway 50. Nightly rates start at $104.

Park Tahoe Inn

4011 Lake Tahoe Boulevard
South Lake Tahoe, CA 96150
Tel: (530) 544-6000
sales@parktahoe.com

Located in central South Lake Tahoe, the Park Tahoe Inn
is a pet-friendly hotel that is close to most everything. Just
across from Heavenly Village, this place is truly a sweet
deal. The hotel has queen-sized beds, free wifi, private
beach access, an outdoor pool and a bubbling hot tub.
Recently renovated, the inn offers all the necessities with
just the right touch of luxury for a modest fee. Nightly
rates begin at $36.

Parkside Inn at Incline

1003 Tahoe Boulevard (SR 28)
Incline Village
Nevada 89451
Tel: (775) 831-1052
Parksideinfo@aol.com

Parkside Inn offers its guests king or queen sized beds,
free wifi, a refrigerator, a 32" TV with cable, forest views,
an indoor pool, a sauna, complimentary continental
breakfast, and a pleasing décor. The location is superb for
a visit to Incline Village, whether you visit during the
summer or the winter season. Nearby establishments
include casinos, beaches, restaurants, and shopping
centers. Prices are around $100 a day.

Places to Eat & Drink

Capisce

178 Hwy 50 Ste A, Zephyr Cove, NV 89448
Tel: (775) 580-7500
http://www.capiscelaketahoe.com

This delightful family-owned Italian restaurant is located
right off Hwy 50, near to the Nevada Beach State Park.

Try the authentic Italian pastas and pizzas and order your food "family-style". The restaurant is closed on Mondays. They are open for dinner from 5pm-10pm. Must try dishes include the steaks, Ravs pasta, and for dessert try the Capisce's Lake Tahoe Sunny Buns. Prices for main courses range from $11 - $30.

Fireside Pizza Company

The Village at Squaw Valley,
1985 Squaw Valley Rd.,
Olympic Valley, CA, 96146
Tel: (530) 584-6150
www.firesidepizza.com

The Fireside Pizza Company claims to be the best gourmet pizza restaurant in Squaw Valley. Aside from their mouthwatering pizzas they also serve chicken, pasta and dessert. It is good place for families as they have a kids menu. Try their Fireside Pizza or a simple and reliable Pepperoni pizza. You can build your own pizza and they also serve gluten-free pizzas. Prices range from $5 - $20.

Scusa! Italian Ristorante

2543 Lake Tahoe Blvd., near Silver Dollar Ave.,
South Lake Tahoe, CA 96150
Tel: (530) 542-0100
www.scusalaketahoe.com

Open daily for dinner from 5pm – 10pm, this Italian restaurant offers elegance at a moderate price. Enjoy an al fresco dining experience under the night sky while digging into their Italian cuisine. The house favorites include classic lasagna, grilled chicken and ravioli. The prices are around $15-$20 per main course.

Jason's Beachside Grille

8338 N. Lake Blvd., Hwy. 28,
Kings Beach, CA 96143
Tel: (530) 546-3315
www.jasonsbeachsidegrille.com

Jason's Beachside Grille offers a lakeside dining experience and is open from 11am daily. It has a giant salad bar which also includes a variety of fruits, vegetables and pasta salads. Jason's is a family restaurant that offers a kids menu and a full bar. There are 16 types of burgers on the menu and a favorite dish is the Barbecued Baby Back Ribs. Lunch prices are around $7 - $11 while dinner prices are from $18 – $21.

Cantina

765 Emerald Bay Rd.,
Hwy. 89, at 10th St.,
South Lake Tahoe, CA, 96150
Tel: (530) 544-1233
www.cantinatahoe.com

Cantina is a favorite bar and restaurant in South Lake
Tahoe and is an excellent place to "hang out" and enjoy
good food. It stock over 30 beers and has one of the best
Mexican menus in the area. It has 3 televisions sets that
provide entertainment as well as a patio for outside
dining. Price range from $4 - $15.

Places to Shop

Don Cheepo's

3349 Lake Tahoe Blvd,
South Lake Tahoe, CA 96150
Tel: (530) 544-0356

This is one of the best places in South Lake Tahoe to buy
snow gear. The store provides excellent service at good
prices and the owner is knowledgeable.

Truckee Shops

10065 Donner Pass Road,
Truckee, CA
Tel: (530) 587-8808

There are a lot of good stores in the Truckee shopping district on the way into Lake Tahoe. Listed below are some affordable places:

Forget-Me-Not

10228 Donner Pass Road,
Truckee, CA 96161

A stylish little store that offers women's clothes and accessories as well as gift items that you can buy at good prices.

Niche Boutique

10164 Donner Pass Road,
Truckee, CA 96161
Tel: (530) 587-3100

More affordable than many stores in Truckee, this quaint store offers women's clothing and accessories.

Cobblestone Center

North Lake Boulevard, Tahoe City, CA
Tel: (530) 583-1580
http://www.cobblestonetahoe.com/

In Tahoe City, the Cobblestone Center sets the bar when it comes to the Tahoe City shopping mall experience. The design of the mall is funky and it would be worthwhile to take a look and see what kind of bargain you can find. They also have restaurants, health and wellness stores, as well as snow equipment rental shops. Also look for the famous Tahoe City landmark, the Cobblestone Clock Tower.

Boatworks Mall

760 North Lake Boulevard
Tahoe City, CA 96145
Tel: (530) 583-1488
http://www.boatworksmall.com/

This two-storey mall has plenty of good shops and restaurants. It is easily accessible via the Tahoe Area Regional Transit (TART) and by car and they provide free parking. The stores range from clothes to toys to jewelry. Visit two of the funky clothes boutiques: Tahoe T-Shirtery (Tel: (530) 583-7495) and Fine 'N Funky (Tel: (530) 583-1400; www.shopfinenfunky.com)

The Shops at Heavenly Village

1001 Heavenly Village Way,
South Lake Tahoe, CA 96150
Tel: (775) 265-2087

You cannot visit South Lake Tahoe without looking around the Shops at Heavenly Village. Some stores may be a little pricey but you will find ones that offer more affordable deals. Aside from the retail stores there are also a number bars and restaurants for you to enjoy. Looking around is always a pleasure. **All About Tahoe** (Tel: (877) 444-8044) offer the personalization of your Lake Tahoe memorabilia. It is a good place to shop for a gift. **Shirt Off My Back** (Tel: (530) 544-3216) offer factory/outlet prices for Lake Tahoe branded apparel and headwear. It's also a great place to shop for a souvenir or a gift.

CPSIA information can be obtained
at www.ICGtesting.com
Printed in the USA
BVHW04s0741230918
528265BV00020B/471/P